Salute to the Remains of a Peasant

By
Oumar Farouk Sesay

PublishAmerica
Baltimore

First printing

At the specific preference of the author, PublishAmerica allowed this work to remain exactly as the author intended, verbatim, without editorial input.

ISBN: 1-4241-7388-4 (softcover)
ISBN: 978-1-4489-0471-6 (hardcover)
PUBLISHED BY PUBLISHAMERICA, LLLP
www.publishamerica.com
Baltimore

Printed in the United States of America

Dedication

DEDICATED TO ALL THOSE TRANSFORMED TO MONUMENTS AND METAPHORS DURING THE DECADE OF WAR IN SIERRA LEONE

Table of Contents

Introduction

For much of its troubled post-independence history, one of the many casualties of Sierra Leone's demise from promise to disaster has been the non-existence of an artistic environment for musicians, writers and painters to express their talents. Whereas other West African states like Mali, Senegal, and Ghana are famous for their distinctively glorious music, fine art and, to a lesser extent, their literary output, the same cannot be said of Sierra Leone. This is surprising considering that the written word has flourished in Sierra Leone for well over two hundred years.

In the beginning there was promise, but since 1961, good newspapers would appear only to die later; great schools, established during the nineteenth and early twentieth centuries, went on a step decline in the nineteen seventies, from which they have never recovered. The country's unchallenged primacy in broadcast journalism suffered a similar fate. Now, although there are many newspapers and radio stations, much of what comes from them is so poor as not to warrant a discussion about their usefulness.

As far a contemporary literature is concerned, although there were a few names here and there during the sixties, this art form was never really part of the Sierra Leonean cultural milieu.

Curiously, whereas she was the recipient, and proud interpreter, of an English-style education, that inheritance seemed to have worked against the growth of an indigenous African literature of daring, shaped by the African sense of narrative music, rhythm and multifaceted world view, as occurred in the rest of West Africa. By and large, the schools emphasised a boring English tradition in which literature was to be studied for exams, not written and enjoyed as part of the social and cultural fabric.

The result was that, with the exception of a handful of writers, most of them now in their late greying years, the robust panorama encompassing drama, poetry and fiction, for which the region is noted, never materialised in Sierra Leone.

Fortunately though, probably because of the ability of Sierra leoneans to now travel more widely to other African nations, and vice versa, the richness of an African tradition is beginning to make itself felt in the new literature of Sierra Leone. I say new because the writers now writing, especially the poets have freed themselves of the iambic pentameters, rhymes and metaphors of their earlier compatriots; much of whose writings were copycat varieties of the English poetry they had learned in school.

Poetry demands freshness and urgency. It is the ability of a writer to use words with vigour, magic, daring and, ultimately, create music in verse. It is the gift of the healer to express in words what ails the wounded and the despairing. Given the spontaneity of many West African art forms, poetry should be as robust and soaring as the region's dazzling musical forms. This is the gift of the Nigerians and Senegalese; it is the magic of the Malians, so that, today, the world had come to recognise a particular sound or literature from those countries.

Now, slowly, we are witnessing the emergence of a younger crop of Sierra Leonean poets—Gbanabom Hallowell and Oumar Farouk Sesay being two of the most interesting—who are determined to create a poetic renaissance in Sierra Leone. The present volume is Oumar Sesay's first and is a fine example of the many styles and influences that have gone into shaping this poet's voice.

Many of the poems are testimonies to what has happened in Sierra Leone in the past fifteen years: the psychological traumas resulting from a failed future, the collapse of a national ethos, the carnage of war, the upheaval of its people and more. But this is not merely a volume about disasters, as that is not the sole business of poetry. From the vantage point of an observer—one crucially sensitive to the hopes and exhilaration of his people—there are flashpoints of serenity, joy and meditation on love.

To read Oumar Sesay is to be reminded that, at the end of the day, a poet's duty is not merely to sing about his or her own trials, but to make accomplice all the complex destinies of those around him:
Here, in this poem entitled 'DREAM,' is an example of Sesay at his best:

'Don't let go your dream,
Cling to it, like a mother
In a war-ravaged land
Will cling to a dying child

Don't let go your dream
Clutch at it, like a drowning man
Will do a straw.

Don't let go your dream,
Embrace it, like a love-starved
Romeo will do to a Juliet.'

The beauty of this poem is that whereas the social context is undoubtedly that of war, there is the refreshing tone of hope, the irreducible reminder of how we must never give up on life; not even when all seems lost. It is an exhortation to man to never stop dreaming or loving. With this volume, I predict Oumar Sesay will help usher in the renaissance in Sierra Leonean poetry so long overdue.'

-SYL CHENEY-COKER

Posters

Vote for the son of the soil
Vote for the poor man's son
Behold: a feudal lord in serf mask
A bastard son of the soil marred
To rape mother's womb
For champagne and gold.

Scenes

Streak of hunger, wrinkles of strain
They Make spiders' webs on the pained faces
While human remains litter the streets
From fractional death and slave chains
And pot bellied men in limousines splash water
On shadows struggling in queues for crumbs
Dogs lurk in corners to kill the lumps

At Tellu Bongor

Dedicated to the 63 people massacred by RUF rebels at Tellu
Bongor

What prowls like a hungry tiger in the Gola forest of my mind
Is rage nursed to puncture your heart for raping your mother at
Tellu Bongor.
What rages like a rabid dog in the dustbin of my mind is rebellion,
against you for butchering you father at Tellu Bongor
What fires like a hurricane in the savanna of my mind is disdain
for you for entombing the wombs at Tellu Bongor.
Nurtured by pain termites gnaw the walls of my mind
And the blisters on my hands, red like the intifadas in the Gaza
Strip
Burn from touching the limbs that you dismembered at Tellu
Bongor
And a hungry lion in the kailahun of my mind is enraged
To snatch your galled heart at Tellu Bongor

No

(On a commission to write a poem of love)

No I cannot write it here
That poem that will
Scoop the mind-fields of
Mindless warmongers
Munching souls of mortals like
A monster, for muddled up cause.

No I cannot write it here
That poem that will diffuse
Nuclear bombs, stop arms escalation
Knock of scud weapons like
Patriot missile.

No I cannot write it here
That poem that will clean
Hate ridden hearts with a
Love that has no
Color, creed and race.

No I cannot write it here
That poem that will be poor
In verse but rich in love
For all of God's creation

No I cannot write it here
Those poetry children portray
In playgrounds, birds sing in shrubs.

No I can not write it,
But I want you to read it
In the childhood anthology
It is there, the poetry of love
That brought us here.

I can see it in that child
Feel it in her smiles
Sense it in her chemistry
Hear it in her breath.

Yet I refuse to write it
But I want you to read it
Read the rhyme scheme
In the rhythmic movement of
Their feet in the playground.

Read the similes in their
Smiles, and the metaphor
In their mood.

Read it, it is there
The poetry of love
But I cannot write it.

For Mansion Sake

With guns pouring blood
Golding's children scribble hate
On the Liberian drenched diary
To blur posterity's eye
For mansion's sake

Stabbed the wounds Pour acid
Torture, mutilation and rape of
Mother Liberia
While suckling nymphs were plucked
From their mother's nipple and
Crushed of lives
For mansion sake

Like hawks, the death angels clad
In white robes soared to seek chicken in a
Cannibalize mother Liberia
And seasoned cannibals for dollars' sake
Raised barreled olive leaves

Once Again

This wound in the Earth
Is the grave of my heart
I traverse a landscape
Stripped of its own heart
In search of hope

A scar in the Earth
Marks the grave of my soul
I roam with a soulless
Body searching for my soul
In the womb of the earth, my life is a compass
drifting like driftwood
In turbulent waters

A site on the vast Earth
Blurs my sight
I grope in dens and graves
Without a sight
For Oumou Kultum Sesay
Buried in the earth's womb
And search for her likes
To mother me once again

Ghetto Boy

Wrenched from the ghetto rife with stench
He strive to wriggle out of the trenches
But was rigged before his birth
To reside in graves made rugged
By disciples of naked greed

Tears from mourners
Make moist the earth
For souls scorned
By mortal gods to be buried in uncelebrated

Morns drawn the groans of mothers in labor
As they push their off spring
To the clutches of crucified humanity
To cross across unknown

Independence

She came drench in a bloody placenta
With an uncut cord
Gasping midwives who performed
The liberation caesarean without
Anesthetics in an open theatre
Gazed at the enigma:
The dumb lumps named
The free but chained
The Independent but dependent
The aged but young
The weaned but suckling
The born but unborn
I-N-D-E-P-E-N-D-E-N-C-E

Free at Last

"...When we allow Freedom to ring...from
every village and every Hamlet, from every
city, we will be able to speed up that
day when all of God's children—Black men
and White men, Jewish and Gentiles, protestants
and Catholic, will be able to
join hands sing in the words of the
old Negro spiritual!
Free at last! Free at last!
Thank God all mighty we are Free at last!
    Martin Luther King (Jr.)

Free at last
On the American screen
Where I strive to magnify
The image of the criminal
Lurking in the American mind.

Free at last
In prison and corrective institution
Where I acquire the equivalent
Of a Harvard degree and membership
In the alumni club.

Free at last
In the streets of Harlem
Where my brain is encased,
in a cocaine prison
Wardened by abuse

Free at last
In the sub-Way of New York
Where old ladies clutch
At their bags and gasp
In fear of my black skin.

Free at last
On the Street of Washington
Where I liberally hire my body to all races
For Big-Mac, and Kentucky Fried chicken

Free at last
In the American Psyche
Where I stride, gun in hand,
A billboard, advertising crime

Middle Passage

They come again
After the Middle Passage
On a Paid passage
To Goree, where centuries ago
They passed through passages
To the Middle Passage

They come again
After the Middle Passage
To Goree, with cameras in the studios
Of their minds capturing
images like the
Goree captives' centuries ago

They come again
After the Middle Passage
On a paid Passage
To Goree with chains,
Chaining their rage
Neck to neck
Ankle to ankle
Like slaves in Goree
Four hundred years ago.

They come again
After the Middle Passage
On a paid Passage to Goree
In their womb they carry
The agony of a race
Born four hundred years ago

They come again
After the Middle Passage
on a paid passage
To Goree, tossing tokens
To slaves of dreams
Drench in despair
Like slaves centuries ago
They come again
After the Middle Passage
On a paid Passage
To Goree starring at
The sea soaking memories
Of cruelty to mankind

They come again
After the Middle Passage
On a paid Passage
To Goree with a
Halo cry of reparation
Like the cries of agony
Four hundred years ago.

Inspired by a visit to Goree Island in Senegal, one of the Island used as a transit point for slaves it is reported that millions of slaves died in Goree island during slavery.

The Cry

Rage
Despair
Anguish
Pain
Congealed in the chambers of her soul
As she writhes in the holes of Bunce Island

From the torment of her soul
To the pain of her ovaries
A cry of anguish was born

The cry sucks strength
From the gall of her despair
Ebbs through the tides
Strikes her vocal cords
And explodes into the air
Drenching the cacophony of groans

The Girl slave pants
Like a mother in labor
In the slave house
Where the rape of her humanity
Gave birth to the cry
Her cry mingles
With cries of yesterday
Conspires with sand storm

To torment desert Arabs
The cry drifts in the wind
Unleashing storms
Across oceans

Lashing volcanoes
Takes a sigh in play grounds
Before charging to the Ruffian killing fields

The girl perished
The cry survives her mortality
Hers the Eve of cries
The cry of a century
Drilled though the ears of a poet
The poet packages:
The torment, the pain, and the cry
The cry a verse
The verse a poem
A poem of pain

The girl who cried
Died long ago
In the Middle Passage
Survived by a cry
Perhaps she was born
For just this cry
And the poet
For just this poem

Introduction

I am neither a dollop of dung to be dumped
Nor
A grave of Marx, Mill, Lenin or Locke
Nor
A specimen in a global laboratory
Nor
A drug addict to be intoxicated with toxic waste
Nor
An unclaimed legacy to be plundered and blundered
Nor
A cheap prostitute on lease to wanton men
Nor
A cradle to nurse ideologies
Nonetheless
Am Africa
The cradle
The womb
The breast

The Woman Who Danced

A bundle of hope, a baggage of despair
Braves the cultural Babel and assaults the stage
Shuffling her age and surfing her soul
For the drifting soul of her ancestry in Afro beats.
She wriggles and writhes through the ring of rhythm
Scarred like the sole of her soul.

Alone in the crowded stage of Zanzibar
She danced for the African woman
Trapped in the corn fields of Africa
Suckling and sucking
She danced for the African woman shackled
In the shambles of western glamour
For whom the drum beats no more.

Her contours contract to the rhythm
And rhythm conjure her contours
Unifying her spirit to the ancestral soul
Oozing from the African drums
Her feet pour on the stage like libation
For the ancestor who died for the survival
Of Seigureh and drums in Carnegie Hall.

Decibel after decibel of her heritage
Congealed in melody drill through her ears
Prick her neurons and stimulate her sinews
The woman danced for a generation of women
Who labored and died without a song
Without a dance

The Child Who Danced

I was the Poster child
In your posterity posture
That gave pulse to your
Independence debate at Lancaster House

I was the child
Draped in rags
Adorned with hunger
Infested by pests
Consumed by ignorance
Who danced in celebration
Of the new dawn

I was the child who believed
The slogans in radio slots
Free education!
Free medical!
Paved roads!

I was the manifesto child in the cover of the book
Smiling to the rising sun
I waited for the utopia
And I waited
Then
I became the infant mortality child
Embedded in scam statistics
To solicit funds.
I became the poster child
For the wrongs of my Sierra Leone

Then

I became a man
With no education
With low life expectancy
An angry man

Shooting verses at vices
I fired volleys of bullets at robed vultures
They called me a rebel.
But I was only the little child
Who danced barefooted for the promise
They made to me on Independence Day.

POEM INSPIRED BY AMINATA' FORNA'S MEMOIRS THE DEVIL
THAT DANCED ON THE WATER

Lines

Date lines
Time lines
Dead lines
Front lines
Borderlines
Sidelines
Guidelines
Headlines
Punch lines
Bottom lines
Lifelines
Underlined
By lines

Fair Trade

We return to the auction block
Clutching the toil of our soil
And the soul of our toil
Waiting for the hammer
Just as we waited on the auction block
Of the New World in by gone years

We return to the auction block
With the sweat of our toil
Crying against injustice
Just as we cried in the slave house of Elmina

We slouch with sacks
Of devalued cocoa and coffee
Just like we paraded in shackles
With our devalued humanity
In the slave market of North Carolina

We return to the auction block
Banging the doors of G8
For debt relief
Just like we banged the
Dungeons of Goree
For our freedom

We return to the world trade
With mosaic of scars
Stitched on new wounds
On the canvass of our skin

Just like the whip scars
Left on our skin
In the sugar fields

Schipol Airport (On Trasit)

Debris of a Babel tower
Spill like splinters
In the sprawling lounges of Schipol
With bags and burdens
Acting the biblical doomsday
They batter coins for goodies
And tongues for directions
Unknown to computer monitors.

Public Notice

This is private property belonging to poetry
Any unauthorized idea or word
That trespasses this poetry field will be arrested
And prosecuted in a poetic court
Sentenced to serve eternal time with hard labor
In a poem wardened by metaphors
Only to be paroled for good conduct
In a half way house with a number
Before released to acres of minds with a stigma
Like Thomas Gray's ex-convict;
"The curfew tolls the knell of the parting day"
From the maximum prison
Of Elegy in a Country Church yard

I Write What I Feel

No one feels the pangs
Of a mother in labor
But the mother in labor

No one feels the grip
Of the hangman's rope
But the hanged man

No one feels the strains
Of mending soles
But the mender of soles

No one feels the burden
Of a luggage

But the carrier of the luggage

No one feels the nagging
The throbbing, the probing,
The gnawing, the curiosity
The anxiety on the
Mind of the writer
But the writer

No one feels what I write
No one tells me what I write
I write what I feel.

Make Me the Poet

Make me the poet
That will write the poetry
Of your beauty blooming
Like flowers in spring.

Make me the poet
That will write the poetry
Of your heart sprouting
With love like a fountain.

Make me the poet

That will traverse rich
And wretched landscape
Like a roaming poet reading
Your poetry to nature

Make me the poet
That will plunge into the
Depth of the sea to read
Your poetry to the ocean

Make me the poet
That will soar like
An eagle to the sky above
To sing your poetry to the galaxy

Make me the poet
That will tell it all in a poem.

When My Pen Pours Poetry

When my pen pours poetry
It spurs my pulse to pour
The passion of my soul
To make ink for my pen

When my nib strikes the
Paper, it leaves scars of devastations
In the heart of the paper
For posterity to see

When my pen pours poetry
It crushes the gates of my
Heart and lets out my
Pain for the
Monsters that munch
The mutton and leave
The bones for the mongrels

When my pen pours poetry
It tramples on the minefields
Of my mind and mark me
For a mission

When my pen pours poetry
It pours it for a social change.

He Did Not Die That Day

When the tale of the toll
Of the war was told
In the warmth of our room
My husband folded the sleeves of his Ronko
Sharpened his spear
Smeared mafoi on his body
Beat his chest
Spewed honey bees
The lion growled;
"I will die for your honor"

When the renegade came
Violence galore;
Looting my honor
Raping my dignity
Entombing my womb
He did not die that day
His heart pounds
Stomach of beehive rumbles
His Ronko and spear
Behind the door
Next to the bottle of Mafoi
Remained untouched
He shriek under the bed
As the renegades killed my honor

But he did not die that day
Yet he is dying everyday
For not dying that day

Ronko—Traditional cloth made of rough cotton and imbibed with charms to protect the owner
MAFOI-A themne people word for a concoction of herbs with healing and protective powers used by traditional warriors

Prompters

Prompters:　Devalue your currency
Actors:As a panacea to the ills of
This country I am proud
To announce that the
National currency has
Been devalued forthwith.

Prompters:　Float your currency
Actors:Countrymen in our
Endless search for a
Solution to our Economic
Woes we have decided
To float the national currency.

Prompters:　Remove subsidies and redundant workers
Actors:My people, building an
Emergent nation like ours
Demand selfless sacrifice.
We must be ready
To pay the price
For development We
Have therefore decided
To remove subsidy on
Rice and petrol and to
Lay off forty five percent
Of the work force

Prompter: Implement Structural Adjustment Programmed
Actors: Patriots, the seriousness of
Our problems has forced
Us to implement a comprehensive
Structural adjustment programme

We must all tighten our
Belts for the rough times ahead

People: No school! No college! No subsidy! No work!

Prompters: Atmosphere not conductive
Actors: Fellow citizens, the riotous
Conduct of some self-styles
Champions of Nationalism
Who claimed to be protesting against
The austerity measures is
Tarnishing the image of the
Country and driving investors away
As custodian of the
Constitution, I therefore ask
Members of the armed forces
To restore order by force of arms
Because internal vigilance is the price we got to pay for our liberty

Prompters: am leaving because you are not democratic
Actors: E.........................

Actors

Actors costumed in rags
Garments, masks and robes
Assault the round stage

Abusing entries and exits
Running from the wings
To cram at centre stage
Blocking and off-staging each other

To act;
Like judges
Like gods
Like academicians
Like rich men
Like slaves
Like actors
Acting an endless script
Ridden with plots
Without directors

Speeches

Their mills milled out
Fricatives and plosive
To form words.
Words pieced together to sentences.
Sentences stringed to speeches
Delivered to sooth
The mutilated hearts of
Despairing peasants
To scoop the mind fields
of the mindless
To diffuse the pulsating
Time bomb in the pulse
Of the down trodden.

Speeches were delivered
To fit the fetters of slavery,
prolong misery, and give
A dint of humane color
To the dehumanized

Like alkaline
In a beaker filled with acid
The speeches neutralized the acid of hate, and boldly held
Them and their offspring
To the slavery of the mind
The soul and the body.

Wounds

Stinking festering wounds snare
At us everywhere
In the heart of our treasury
Wounds every where
In the lyrics of our lullabies
Wounds everywhere

In the core of colleges
Wounds everywhere

In the womb of our tombs
Wounds everywhere

In the mines of our minds
Wounds everywhere

In the essence of our existences
Wounds everywhere

Stinking festering wounds
Oozing puss

Ma Musa

A conspicuous sprout
From the thicket
Smiling and wooing
The landscape
In the day
The sprawling green
The toiling peasants
The teeming traffic
Snob the suitors smile.
The shroud of the
Dead day is torn
Apart from Gbakanda's
Ancestral greetings
The rhythm of drums
Summon the choir of
Crickets and birds
To sing a lullaby that
Cradles the village to sleep

Like an off note
Macadam's tyrant shatter
The melody and now
The village is awake
And the toiling starts

The suitor is snubbed.

Gbakanda is a name of a theatre group renowned for cultural performances

Africa

As the torrent of August pour,
She weeps for her scar spangled
Body marks of rappers
Who sprawled her on fetters
And plunder her womb.
And stuff opium to seduce her battered sensation
She wails and writhes
In the mud muddled
With blood and semen
Oozing from her trespassed
Property,
Sex maniacs
Groan with ecstasy to every
Plunge and plunder.
She weeps like August rain
As puppets mock her
Rescue to thrill her off springs.
They plunge again with zeal
And gusto in her blistered canal
Reducing her speech to mourns
Music of romance for the maniacs
Wrinkles like yawning gutters
in August's torrent
Cross her mangled face
As she screams at the assorted queue of
Rappers, brandishing their weapons
Waiting for the onslaught;
She mourns and groans
For the rape of her
Pride and bleed like the August
Torrent that eroded the land

I Want to Cry

I want to cry
A cry of pain
Panting in perils
Painted like paradise

I want to cry
A cry of anguish
Anchoring pent up anger
For the devil Angels
Robbing and raping humanity

I want to cry
A cry of solitude
Felt in the servitude
Of the Mongols
I want to cry
A cry of agony
For the trivialities
Spun to give credit
To the futility of life

I want to cry
A hallow and harrowing cry
For the hollowness
Of wallowing in a hollow world

I want to cry
A shattering cry
Shaking the shackles
Of a shambled world

Gone

(For Ibrahim khalil Dahayan Sesay)

Gone without white hair
Gone without a walking stick
Gone without a wrinkle
Gone with a dream
Just gone without a signal

Publish Me

Publish me
Or I perish
For I pour my blood
And soul on papers
That perished
Like I perished
Unpublished

Dogs

Sprawling and snarling in slums
Their blood smeared fangs,
Flash like carnivorous carnivals
To dine on frozen flesh of under dogs.

Read

Read and tag it poetry
Read and christen it prose
Read and label it drama
Read and call it poetic prose
I just scribbled the nagging
In me for the shrinking
Flora and fauna stunted
By the man made sun.

Dream

(DEDICATED TO TUDADU JARIA SESAY)

Don't let go your dream,
Cling to it, like a mother
In a war ravaged land
Will cling to a dying child.
Don't let go your dream
Clutch at it, like a drowning
Man will do to a straw

Don't let go your dream
Embrace it, like a love
Starved Romeo will do to a Juliet.

Don't let go your dream
Suck it like a breast starved
Child will to her mother's nipple.

Don't let go your dream
Cling, clutch, embrace and suck
Till you perish of flourish with it.

Don't let go you dream.

Poetry

Pour it everywhere
On everything
On whatever
Any how, wherever
And call it, poetry
So long as it comes from the heart

Metal Coffins

Crooked crawling coffins
Crammed with corpses,
Certified by cops,
Collided with other coffins
In cemeteries devouring corpses

Beggars

Beggars in uniforms beg
From beggars in chains
Beggars in chains beg
From beggars in rags
Beggars in rags beg
From beggars in garments
Beggars in garments beg
From beggars in robes
Beggars in robes beg
From the white gods

Desert Storm

Folly of flagged fools
Fan flames of fury
With blood and sweat
Of toiling peasants to
Feed a starving ego.

Folly of flagged fools
Fling agonized hearts
In forlorn lands to nurture
And nurse olive trees
With missiles and mines

Folly of flagged fools
Sprinkle human manure on
Impoverished deserts, and irrigate
With water sprouting from
Mortal fountains to grow
Olive seeds in the desert

Folly of flagged fools
Build castle with Arabian sand.

It Is Raining Again

It is raining again
Just like yesterday's rain
It tears through the latch
And drips on the thatch
Thuds and thaw hearts

Fossilized with differed dreams
Draining like rain to the stream
It is raining
Thuds, thaws and drains
Into drainages with differed dreams
Shattered by agony into seams

It will rain again
On our coffined remains
And they will cuddled our living remains
Pour dreams in their wombs
While we shiver in tombs
But the dream in today's womb
Will be cold in tomorrow's tomb
And dreams will still pour in wombs
As it rains again

Raining again
We cuddled their living remains
Warm as their cold tombs
And pour dreams in their wombs
And dreams that will drain
Into the drains as tomorrow's rain

May 25th

I pour tears like torrent of rain
For the torturers tearing to shreds
The bonds of my country
Like the tangled shreds
Of their bondage on May 25th

I mourn
For the gang rape of my wife
Raped and killed
Killed and raped
On May 25th

I rage like an inferno
Guttering to ashes the avalanche
That swept the carcass of my dreams
On May 25th
I growl like a Mangy dog
For the mongrel
Who devoured the mangled remains
Of my son on May 25th
I groan like a dying nation
Bayoneted to death on May 25th

On September 4th

Twenty-one people killed
At Mabala Slum on September 4th
They were killed not by stray bullets
Fired by the Junta.
Nor
By ECOMOG
Jets firing at Junta
But
They are dead fired at on September 4th
Yet
Neither Junta
Nor ECOMOG killed them
But
They are dead and bleed
At the slums of Mabala
With fresh wounds
Their
Mangled bodies on the wreckage
Of their homes, underneath the cinders
Of their dreams and mourned
By surviving corpses

They died long ago
Before September 4th at Mabala
Killed by a junta that fired
Stray policy through barrels
Of greed and terror
They were killed long ago
When robed vultures

Masqueraded as rulers

To devour their essence
Like the carcasses of sheep
They died on the day

When nepotism replaced meritocracy
And sycophancy guised as virtue
They died long ago and were buried
In a mass grave at Mabala slums

Yet on September 4th
An other junta exhumed and
Killed them again and again
Like they were killed yesterday

Mabla: An inner city slum settlement in Freetown
ECOMOG: The intervention forces of the west Africa economic committee
during the war in Sierra Leone

On This Spot

Come my son
Come! Come! Come!
This is the spot
The very spot

On 'sewa's' edge
On this 'theren'
Here in this spot
   She was killed
Killed! Killed! Killed!
With a 'Kalashnikov'
Shot with a gun
Just a rebel
With a gun
And a bullet
And a twisted mind
She was killed

Killed, dead deceased
On this spot
On this edge
She was ripped with a bayonet
Up middle, bottom
She was ripped
With a bayonet
A poisoned knife
On gun's edge
On sewa's edge
On sanity's edge

On this spot

Here she was wrenched
From the womb
Like a fetus

A denied fetus
On the surgeon's table
Crushed and splashed
On this theren
Spilling blistering yolk
On blood drenched

Theren to make a tapestry
Like abstract patterns
On a canvass
Abstracting the abstractness
We called life
On this edge
She was killed
Killed with a gun
Ripped with a bayonet
Before the pangs
The birth pangs
Preceding the pangs
Of your pangs

Come my son
Come! Come! Come!
Here she was killed with her dreams
And hopes; killed with a gun
A gun

A bullet
A bent mind
She was killed
Before the pangs on this spot
Killed! Killed! Killed!
Come my son

This is you
The blood dots
On this theren

Glowing like an abstract masterpiece

This is you
The poet in the pattern
The metaphor in the splash
This is you killed on sanity's edge

SEWA: A river in eastern Sierra Leone
Theren: Refers to a rock in the local themne language in Sierra Leone

Prime Citizens

PRIME CITIZENS
Primed at the peak
Peeping at pigs prowling
In impoverished pens
For peas to feed piglets

PRIME CITIZENS
Perched on paradise
Peeping at pawns
Perishing in purgatory
For the sin of passivity
PRIME CITIZENS
Enthroned on thrones
Throwing trash in bins
For human trash to trace
PRIME CITIZENS
Grin with satisfaction
As grafted beings
Crawl to gratify them

PRIME CITIZENS
Safe at the summit
Signing death sentences
Of sinners who sinned
Against the single, sacred sin

Revolution of Revulsion

Contrived at Kalashnikov's crack
Conceived at bayonet's edge
Born on the run
Named on the wayside
Marred at birth
Smeared for life
Marked and marketed for nickels
Snuffed out with Kalashnikov's crack
In a revolution of revulsion

.

Fanatics

False fraternity framed
On a feeble handshake
Fashioned on a religion
With a God chained
To distortion, by wretched
Armies chanting chants of
Cheating, teaching cheats
To chant and cheat
Ticketing religion
For checks and politics

The Lone Drum

Embalmed bodies
Mummified souls
Cursed ghosts
Dumb lumps
Dance to the melody
Of the lone drum
When it beats

Still Birth

The day the bombs fell
Like hale from above
A poet and a mother were in labor

Her fist clenched, teeth gritted
Her face contorts in labor and gasps
As the nurse stands at her feet with a laurel
Counting the contractions
And yelling "push" "push"

The poet clenched his soul
His heart palpitated like the mother laboring next door
He heard the midwife yelling as the muse
Urged him to pour poetry for posterity

Yet his heart was stuck
Like a caged bird
With a muffled song
In the wilderness of his mind
Starving his verses of images

The mother pushed
The poet mused
She breathed in gasps
He gasped in breathes
The nursed wedged the faucet inside her
She yelled in pain

The muse grabbed the concept
Of his poem
Chiseled it to a metaphor
The contraction climaxed
Sweat poured from her brow she pushed

His thoughts contracted as images
Kick at the wall of his mind
He sighed and pressed the nib on the sheet
She grabbed the sheet in her clenched fist and pushed
The baby's head emerged
Like a submarine
The muse descended like a free bird
The mood soared
Alas! The voice of the renegades;
Bullets clatter like metal rain
The poet died
The poem a still birth
The mother died
The child a still birth
The survivors survived
A stillbirth

The Ogoni Nine

A minute silence
For the Ogoni nine
Silenced for eternity
For echoing the agony
Of the Ogonies

A minute silence
For Ken Sara Wiwa
Silenced for shattering
The spilling slime
Of agony in Ogoni land
A minute silence
For the savage silence
Soiling the Ogoni sanity
Like the shell sewage
Spilling over Ogoni land
A minute silence
In salute of Sanni's
Sleaze for slime
Spilling over Ogoni land
A minute silence
For diplomatic silence
Sanctioning Sanni's slaughter
In the slaughter house
Of Ogoni land
A minute silence
For the deafening silence
Pitching to a crescendo
With the groans of silence

Ringing like a funeral dirge
In the grave yard of Ogoni land

A minute silence
For a voice silenced
Yet echoing in the Ogoni
Of our hearts.

Where no more silencers
Of the silence voice of the
Voiceless can reach it

We sit in that serene Ogoni
Listening to the silenced voice
Of Sara Wiwa shouting sanity
As we observe
A minute silence for the Ogoni nine

The Old Woman

She is perched on a stool
On the edge of the street
Patching corns
Almost at the end of her life

A life sun scorched the patches of her life:
And the morning years of her life
Were eclipsed by the ploughing of a barren field

Those years of unending suffering
Were devoid of suffrage
Now she is perched on a stool's edge
On a street's edge
Patching corns to ease her evening
And she fans the flame on the corncob
With her 'lefa' as the
Wind fans the twilight
Of her years

LEFA: A hand held fan made out of raffia
NOTE: Inspired by an old woman who was patching and selling corns in the
street of Freetown for a living.

Time

Yesterday
As we heard the chiming
To moments
Molded to mosaic
And buried in our past
We put on the mourning robs
To scar the passing moments
And mourn our lives

Hope

Fragments of blasted hope
Clog my mind's alleyway
Smog of charred dreams
Fogs my mind's sphere

Odors of decayed dreams
Infest my mind's nostrils
Debris of shattered spirit
Hunts my mind's cemetery
Like the unborn ghost
Roaming the war fields of
My Sierra Leone

I traverse the terrain of my
Sierra Leone shooting verses
At vices ravaging her

I plough blasted hopes
I mix charred dreams
I sprinkle decayed desires
I plant shattered sprit
To harvest hope
For my Sierra Leone

Yet

Yet we must beg
For crumbs
To feed leaches latching to us
And lynching our
Dreams day after day
Yet we must wait
Wait for droplet of rain
in the August drought
Rain for us to grow crops
And not crumbs
In the harvest season
Yet we must gnaw at knowledge
Like termites on wood
For our urchins
Under the foot of Mount Aureol
Yet we must wait
On the thresh hold of pain
For Doctors to prescribe
Medication as we die
In their laps in the thousands
While they finger our pennies

Yet again we must beg for total death
From renegades doling death to us
As we yearn for total death
To stop the waiting
The crying and the begging

Our cries! A crescendo
Our begging! A chorus
Our waiting! A tenor

Our gnawing! An alto
Our life! A dirge
Yet
We are not heard.

Stone Breakers

A stone on a rock
A hammer sinewed on her trunk
Dreams wedged between rocks
Discordant melody of crushed rocks
Make an orchestra of agony
For the soul of the stone breaker

Piles of broken stones
Rubbles of shattered hopes
Debris of differed dreams
Piled at her feet
Every crushed stone
Is a mile without a milestone
She sits on a rock
Crushing stones with a hammer
As the sun drench away
The morning years of her life

Her stones build castles
But she sleeps with cattle
Dreaming of those castle
Built with her toil

Let Me

For years I frolicked in folly
Fending for frailties on the fringes
Shunning your warmth
Today I return like a prodigal poet
Pouncing at your door to let me muse once more
Shoot missiles of metaphors
Bombs of similes
To shatter into shambles
The shackles on the minds of renegades
Contenting in our discontent
Wedge my nib in their loins
Like the bayonet on innocence's loins
Ripping their entrails for vultures to dine
Steer at the streak of guilt in their eyes
As they beg for death on the gallows of Pademba Prison
Write about the wrath writhing
Inside me like a scorched serpent
For the wretched wreaking havoc
On my mother land
Pour the pulsating pain
In my country's pulse
As she dies of overdose of greed
Rage like a hurricane
Burning to ashes looters
Looting the vaults of my country

Mad Man

(On the highway)

A mad man marauding like a quarry
Beyond the borders of his mind
Unfettered by limitations
Vanquished from the void of vanity
Free like a bird from the cages of expectations
He soars to the apex of freedom in the maze of his mind
Where he mocks our bordered existence
Mad man of Kambia
Clad in winter coat in the sweltering heat of March
He limps with a fractured limb to the edge of the highway
Where his mind cruises in limbo
As he punches the wind like a conjurer
Trying to conjure the world in his image
From the edge of the road he laughs at the madness
Of the travelers on the highway
He waves at passersby Senior men' he calls them
The mad man of Kambia is busy being mad
He forgets to wash
Mad man of Tawuya
He sits on a rock with his head scaffolded on his palm
His mind roaming his ravaged mindscape
Brooding over his fate and the world of edges
He paces his mind peeping at the sane world
He prostrates in prayer
Thanking God for a day of madness
Mad man of Rokupr
He gazed in daze like a medium

His mind in exile
And his body roamed like a zombie
Across the scarred landscape
Passersby gazed at him in daze
But the daze in his gaze streak through the land like lightening
Leaving a trail of daze stricken faces in the township of Rokupr

Mad woman of Rokupr
She is lean and thin
Fed with un-thoughts
A tormented being prowling her mind empty of the world's

Mad man of Sanders Street
On his head gory locks
In his mind gridlocks
His feet pivoted
And his mind in perpetual spin
Like the world around him
Mad man of cotton tree
Ragged in rags
Like the tangled rags of his mind
Riveted in the centre of town
Mocking the wailing sirens
As they celebrate the mad men of Tower hill
Mad man of Tower hill
Housed in sanatorium like mansion
Guided by machine guns
He streaks through town in a motorcade
Heralded by wailing sirens

He conjures the world as a utopia
By punching the wind and shouting slogans
He chairs the conference of mad men in the land

Poem inspired by the increasing number of insane people in post war Sierra Leone

---

TOWER HILL: The seat of power in Sierra Leone
Kambia,Rokupr,Tawuya: towns and villages in the northern province in Sierra Leone
Sanders street: a street in the western end of Freetown the capital of Sierra Leone
Cotton tree: the historic tree in the center of Freetown

Driftwood

The fading warmth of a feeble
Kiss is all I cling to like
A life jacket
As I drift in a foaming
Sea of emotion

I drift like driftwood
To islands without color
Eating decayed fruits
To appease a nagging hunger
For love without color

Salute to the Remains of a Peasant

From a thatched hut of mud
On the fringes of the forest
To an unmarked heap of mud
In the depth of the forest
His mortal mould of mud
Is laid to rest
After a life of unrest in the mud

The Birth of a Poem

At USIS Library I witness
The birth of a poem
I saw Gbanabom
Writhing and twisting in pain
His contours coil and contrast
To the rhythm of his clenched mind
Perception conjugate with conception
The birth pangs
The pain, the pushing
And the pulling
The poem emerged from the womb
Of Gbanabom's mind dripping
Bits by bit on the white sheets

I saw the child suckling
Milk of metaphor
Eating images with water
From the river Rokel
Where U'tamsi washes his hands.

USIS: The United State information service library in Sierra Leone
GBANABOM; A Sierra Leonean poet
Tchikaya U'tamsi: The late great Congolese poet (1931-1988)

Street Scenes

Like images in a poem
They roam the streets
Changing direction at random
In search of direction
In a maze of a heritage
Spanning several epochs

Others walk aimlessly like
Redundant images in poetry
Of survival
Others shed their essence
In the presence of donors
Of shelter and food

They crisscross the street
Like images in a poem
Making a pattern, a theme
And poetry of survival,
With rhyme and rhythm
Harmonizing off beats

Pain

On this scorched landscape
Of my mind
Underneath these concrete slabs
Adorned with epitaphs on mangled tablet
Lay the immortal remains
Of my country's pain

This pain lived a life of neglect
And is survived by post war pain
The pain of panting in penury
In the slums of Kurubay
The pain of a paradise periled
In the rice fields of Mangebureh
The pain of impunity
In the court rooms of justice

Kurubay: Inner City slums in Freetown
Mangebureh: a village in the North of Sierra Leone renown for rice farming

"Hand to Mot"

Gas gulping monsters
Gushing carbon monoxide
Bleaching the ozone layer
Crawl to the city
Choked with wood and coal
Stolen from the forest
In the name of "hand to mot"

Kolosa Kargbo

Removed from our heart's womb
And carried to earth's tomb
By death's cold hand
Starving our hungry land
Of manna from his mind's menu

We ached as death's treachery
Wrenched him from our hearts
And entrenched him
In earth's hollow midst
Abandoning us to wallow
In this hollow world.

Tears mourning the mortal death
Of the immortal KOLOSA
Stream like a canal irrigating
The land of our forlorn hearts
So that flowers with pollen and
Fragrances, deprived like Soweto
Flowers, will grow as an African Heritage
Willed to the Kolosas
Left to die alone in foreign lands unmourned

KOLOSA KARGBO: An established poet and playwright whose play, a political satire titled Poyoton Wahala, paved the way for the introduction of censorship in Sierra Leone in the hay days of the single party. His play on the evils of apartheid—Soweto Flowers—singled him out as an eminent writer during the hay days of theatre in Sierra Leone. He died while in exile in Nigeria

Perhaps

Perhaps we still have time
To fan flames of ethnicity
As the anger of hunger
Eat the sinew of our souls

Perhaps we still have time
To wage war with wagging
Tongues as "Ruffians" burn
Our unborn

Perhaps we still have time
To engage in polemics
As they gang rape
Our mother.

Perhaps we still have space
To press a divide in the
Press as they divide us
In bits in the Gola Forest

Perhaps we still have strength
To mudsling as Ruffians
Fire grenade in our
Kindergartens for sport

Perhaps we still have voices
To harp innuendos as an
Ailing nation wails
In agony

Perhaps we still have time
Like the bleeding ghosts
Roaming the Ruffian
Killing Fields.

Perhaps we are still numb
Like the Mabela Tombs
To the agony of
The people

Perhaps we are still ignorant
Like the Boy soldiers
Of the Bits
Of the May 25th beat

MABALA: An inner city slum in Freetown
RUFFIAN: Refers to the revolutionary united front movement who fought a
bloody war with the state in the 90s

My Will

When I die bury
Me deep in the
Bowls of the earth

Place granite stones on my coffin
Erect your monuments of filth for epitaph.
Or
Cremate my body, sprinkle
The ashes into the sea
Or
Grind the remains of
My mortal mould and
Feed your pigs and soil
Or
Hang my remains on
The cotton tree for
Vultures and flies to feed on
Or
Dissect me and preserve
My entrails and skeleton
In the laboratory
Mark them specimen A and B.
But when I die,
Don't bury my poetry
In the prison of your
Shelves under your beds
In your cockroach
Infested boxes for mice

And cockroaches to dine
Don't pluck the pages of
My poetry to wrap crumbs
Read my poetry
Sing my poetry
Act my poetry
The only legacy
I will leave
To the cruel world

Peddlers

They peddled in the corridors of power
for a pinch of influence
To dangle on pimps
Made limp by lumps
Of lust; pimps who munch
The lunch and leave the crunch
For their slumbering lot in the slums
As peddlers peddle their essence
To powerbrokers for a dime

The World's World

The surge of Emotion
That urges me to plunge
In your hazel world
Is drifting me in a world of warm arms
That re-enkindled the smoldering
Flame of love in my heart
And set my whole self ablaze

A world with kisses
Charged with true love
In defiance of a deceptive world

A world with smiles
Sprouting from the heart's tremor
Mocks the serpent's smiles
It is a world of hazel beauty
Harmonizing with nature
In contrast to a harried and hunted world

A world of love without
Color, race, greed and class

Somalia

The harrowing images of children
Sucking the nipples of deceased mothers
And vultures waiting for dying children
And dogs feasting on living carcasses
Appear daily as flies buzz in celebration
Of human folly

Corpses contend for graves
Dug by living corpses,
And on television monitors
The human farce
Snares at us like a prologue
While combative vampires
Suck the alien blood of corpses
In the grave yard of Somalia

Dele

It not about the death
Of a mortal like the mortals
On obituary pages
Or
Of a hired artist painting
Portraits of dictators for crumbs

Yet it is about the death
Of characters coffined in unfinished plays
Of poems pounded to oblivion deprived of images
Of songs stretched to sorrows never to receive lyrics
Of drums itching to gush out rhythms
Of actors lost on stage waiting for direction
Of a playwright righting a wrong in his writing
Of a plot to un-plot evil

It is about the death
Of a play and a playwright
A poem and a poet
A song and a singer
A direction and a director
An art and an artist
It is about the death
Of Dele Charlie

Dele Charlie: a renowned Sierra Leonean poet, playwright and theatre
practioners who died in the early 90s

Letter to an Imprisoned Journalist

Dear Lansana,

I was told you are imprisoned
For contempt of contempt
But I don't know the prison

Is it the prison where the
Prisoners who imprisoned you are imprisoned?
Or
Is it the prison where paupers
Are poured for the crime of poverty?
Or
Is it the prison where
Human crumbs glamour for crumbs?
Or
It is the prison where the reasoning of prime thinkers is
imprisoned?
Or
Is it the prison of perpetual darkness?
Or
Is it the prison where rappers got raped and savages are severed?
Or
Is it the prison where dogs
And underdogs snarl at each other in dustbins?
Or
Is it the prison where paupers
Are enriched and 'enrichers' beg from paupers?
Or

Is it the prison where mourners mourned the smoldering of their mortal mould?
Or

Is it the prison of the dual sun where one sun creates and the other devastates?
Or
Is it the prison where monuments are erected in honor of thieves and murderers?
Or

Is it the prison of the miraculous lone voice that speaks for the dead, the living and the unborn?
Or
Is it the prison where children
Rape the motherland to quench their lust?
Or is it the prison where dumb
Numb lumps sing songs of praise for their executioners?

Lansana, tell me what prison?
I want to write you a letter.

Yours truly.
Farouk

You Are

(For my wife Fatima Sesay)

You are the paper for my poetry starving for metaphors
You are my poetry beaming with beauty
You are my canvas itching for the caressing strokes of my brush
You are the sculptured marble destined to stay in my heart's museum
You are my play rehearsed to be acted on the stage of my life
You are my blooming flower waiting for my wind to waft your pollen
You are my sweet lyrics waiting for my voice to sing your song
Above all you are simply:
My poetry to be read
My lyrics to be sang
My clay to be molded
My canvas to be painted
My marble to be sculptured
My play to be acted
My pollen to be wafted
You are:
My love, my life
My life, my love

Rebels

A specter of Gloom
Loomed over the horizon
As zombies zoomed
The nation to doom
With the boom boom of bombs

Fired by barren minds
Trapped in the glamour
Of the gloom which loomed like a biblical curse
Over a doomed nation

Mother Earth

Earth my heart
It aches to see your tender
Ozone skin corroded
By corrosive cosmetics
Made to unmake the maker

It aches to see you wailing
And writhing in chlorofluorocarbon gas
Chambers like a captive.

It aches to see your babies sucking methyl chloroform
Sprouting from your
Poisoned breast

It aches to see you bleached
Grayed, aged, withered by
Carbon tetrachloride
Like bleached ebony

It aches to see your form
Deformed and virility
Sterilized like a sex maniac
By surgeons you mothered.

It aches to see your
Womb entombed and cradle graved
By morticians you wombed

VISTA

I saw it all:
The rape,
The reap
The mutilation,
The mutation
The brutality,
The festivity
The love,
The hate
The race
The chase
The illusions
The allusions
I heard it all:
The groans of agony
The gasps of joy
The cries of anguish
The yearning of souls
The yelling of hearts
The wind of change
The storm of deception
I smelt it all:
The toil,
The fragrance
The poverty,
The posterity
The deprivation,
The appreciation
The integration,

The segregation
The greed
The gaps
I felt it all
The roughness,
The smoothness
The chills,
The thrills
The ills
The spills
I tasted it all:
The pains,
The gains
The hemlock
The honey
The poison,
The pollen,
The blood
The bloom
I saw, I heard
I smelt, I felt
I tasted the demise
Of a cherish dream.

Inspired by my first visit to the United State in 1991.

Rest in Peace

They shall no longer
Rest in peace so
Long as the tormentors
Who channeled them
To the tunnel of the
Grave still torment them
In their graves

They shall no longer rest in peace
So long as the landlords who ejected
Them out of existence
Still exhume their bodies
To build monuments of
Their ill-gotten wealth

They shall no longer
Rest in peace so long
As there is yawning
Inequalities in and out of the
GRAVEYARD

To My Wrinkles

Like a full moon
they radiate to light a dark dungeon

But wrinkles of strain
Contours of age and pain
Hallow burrows of sorrow
Crisscross like contours to eclipse the moon
And herald the eclipse of eclipse.

Strasser

(The early years of the coup that over-threw the single party system)

Strasser stormed tyranny's citadel
And wrenched from the tyrant's fists
The wand that transformed

Husbands to husbandry
And wives to whores
And children to chaffs
And teachers to cheats
And paupers to princes
And pressmen to praise singers
And moron to martyrs
And intellectuals to idiots
And homes to hovels
And hospitality to hostilities
And people to pimps
And nation to nothingness

STRASSER: The Soldier who lead the coup that overthrew the single party system in Sierra Leone in 1992.

CPSIA information can be obtained at www.ICGtesting.com
Printed in the USA
BVOW03s1645180814

363275BV00001BA/165/P